let's play
I SPY
Christmas

let's play books by
© Little Moon Joy Co

are you ready to play i spy?

the letters are not in alphabetical order, just like a real game of i spy.

i spy with my little eye, something beginning with...

g

g is for...

gift

i spy with my little eye, something beginning with...

S

S is for...

santa

i spy with my little eye, something beginning with...

P

P is for...
penguin

i spy with my little eye, something beginning with...

r

r is for...

reindeer

i spy with my little eye, something beginning with...

S

S is for...

snowman

i spy with my little eye, something beginning with...

g

g is for...
gingerbread man

i spy with my little eye. something beginning with...

b is for...

bell

i spy with my little eye. something beginning with...

C

C is for...
cupcake

i spy with my little eye, something beginning with...

b

b is for...

bow

i spy with my little eye, something beginning with...

C is for...
candy cane

i spy with my little eye, something beginning with...

n is for the...
north pole

NORTH
POLE

i spy with my little
eye, something beginning with...

S

S is for...

sleigh

i spy with my little eye, something beginning with...

m

M is for...

mug

i spy with my little
eye, something beginning with...

S

S is for...
stocking

i spy with my little eye, something beginning with...

e is for...

elf

i spy with my little eye, something beginning with...

h is for...

hat

i spy with my little eye, something beginning with...

S is for...
snow globe

i spy with my little eye, something beginning with...

C

C is for...

card

i spy with my little eye, something beginning with...

b is for...

bauble

did you have fun
and find all of the
christmas items?

Manufactured by Amazon.ca
Bolton, ON